The Cormorant Hunter's Wife

Other Books in the Alaska Literary Series

Peggy Shumaker, series editor

The City Beneath the Snow, by Marjorie Kowalski Cole (short stories)
The Rabbits Could Sing, by Amber Flora Thomas (poetry)

The Cormorant Hunter's Wife

poems by

Joan Kane

ALASKA
LITERARY
SERIES

University of Alaska Press
Fairbanks

University of Alaska Press
P.O. Box 756240
Fairbanks, AK 99775-6240

Second edition. First edition published in 2009 by NorthShore Press.

Alaska Literary Series

Library of Congress Cataloging-in-Publication Data
Kane, Joan.
The cormorant hunter's wife / Joan Kane. — 2nd ed.
p. cm. — (Alaska literary series)
ISBN 978-1-60223-157-3 (pbk. : alk. paper)
ISBN 978-1-60223-158-0 (electronic book)
I. Title.
PS3611.A5436C67 2012
811'.6—dc23
2011032938

Cover and interior design by Andrew Mendez
Cover art: *What Does It Take For You To See My Heart*, © 2001 by Susie
Silook. Walrus ivory, stomach, and bone; whalebone, seal whiskers,
metal, wood, and beads. Inspired by Salvador Dali's Burning Giraffe.
Photo by Chris Arend, courtesy of Anchorage Museum of History and Art.

This publication was printed on acid-free paper that meets the minimum
requirements for ANSI / NISO Z39.48–1992 (R2002)
(Permanence of Paper for Printed Library Materials).

Acknowledgments

Grateful acknowledgment is made to the editors of the following, in which versions of these poems have appeared:

Absent magazine: "The White Night Falling" and "Variations on an Admonition"; *AGNI* Online: "Insomnia at North"; *Barrow Street:* "The Slip"; *The Bitter Oleander:* "The Slate Fields"; *Crosscurrents North: Alaskans on the Environment:* "Tiŋmiat," "Due North," and "Withdraw"; *FREEZE:* "Animal Figurine"; *ICE-FLOE:* "A Proposal," "Legend," "Proper," "Ruins," "Rote," "Stative," "The Sunken Forests," "Traveler's Rest," and "Withdraw"; *Northwest Review:* "Anchorage" and "Building the Boats"; *Parthenon West Review:* "The Prodigy" and "The Relation"; *Poetry Daily* website: "Building the Boats."

Table of Contents

One: Antistrophic

The Sunken Forests   5

Rote   7

Legend   8

Insomnia at North   12

The Designation   13

Variable at Prime   14

Proper   15

Stative   16

On the Border of Speech   18

Off Course   19

Ruins   20

Declining the City   21

•

A Proposal   25

Anchorage   26

Placer   27

Building the Boats   28

Exit Glacier   29

Stray and Error   30

The History of Two   32

Ornament   33

Ivu   34

Clear Cut   36

And Other Ruins   37

Laid In   38

Antistrophic   39

Two: Otherwise, Sky

The Prodigy	43
At Bridal Veil Rocks	44
On Eating before Hunting	45
The Greenland Mummies	46
Three Masks	47
Traveler's Rest	50
Variations on an Admonition	51
The Relation	52
Animal Figurine	53
Lost Season	54
The Slate Fields	55
Variable at Nightfall	56

•

Withdraw	59
Tributary	60
The Slip	61
Nelson's Curio	62
Nix	63
Five Stops	64
Fled to the Inlanders	66
Birth at Safety Sound	69
The White Night Falling	70
Haunt	71
The Cormorant Hunter's Wife	72
Theories of Migration	73
Due North	74
Dust in June	75
Tiŋmiat	76

Biographical Note	77

For my family
For the memory of my grandmothers
Taimani qauqrirugut

The Cormorant Hunter's Wife

One: Antistrophic

The Sunken Forests

Just above the waterline
Jut the bone-white
Crowns of drowned trees.
They are bare, they are
Fallen together. I

Scratch the earth
At my feet: I can
No longer draw water.
I recite the ice that has thrown
The river over its banks

And move through a terrain
Of annotations bright,
New and innumerable.
Fire-felled, they gape
At the stump,

Split at the consumed
Root. I will not know how
To forget them
Though I do not know why.
The inlet in the morning—

A thin pan
Inlaid with blue: this I am sure
I have misremembered, for
Always it is a gray
Tint, clay and salt.

The sun is not a dipper
But a jostle in my head.

Rote

It could have been yesterday,
Trying to learn a pattern of water
On water or a road I thought
Prophesied and never found.

Against the backdrop of valley
I lost the flock as it flew past
For no known reason at all,
A sudden and small consolation.

I saw skins hung on rain-wet willows.
I could not fix in mind or memory
The terrible road or where it led.
Perhaps it was sleep moving

Against me, its round hill
Swelling against a flat landscape.
Iris of eye gives evidence of the sea
Growing larger; an obscured sky

Casts over, scatters and rains.
Of a day that will not want to end,
Tomorrow shall be longer.

Legend

I.

I would have been a girl bound in stone, quartz—
Coarse, cracked, and whitening as bone.
Os, echoing away from twin calderas
But for a long string that drew me to the sea.

A sixteen-strand sinnet lain on sand
Marks the rivers unbraiding, knotted,
And plaiting their skeins towards the basin,
Where a red-throated loon, shot through the eye,
Yields his largest rib for an awl.

At our junction a bunch of feathers.
I take a brittle weed in leaf, thumb chert blade
Gray. Our junction a fumarole; when it smokes,
I lose sight of the girl. It is nothing to know
The rift and buckle—

To witness the sun eclipsed for days on end,
The bruised fields redden and freeze.

II.

The sea, then, our garden: a film,
Char of oil on water. A hiss of tides
Run up to that which was burning
And has gone out. A slow

Erosion. It is one thing to
Give oneself to water; I
Wore down to a spur of myself.

A bird with nowhere to land
Alighted on a femur. A terrible need.

The land took a drink of the sea;
Mountain valleys soughed as throats.

She knew of submerged peaks
Recollected in an unheard song,
Seized in a lesser fever.

The induced shore
Keeps still a drowned order.

III.

Meant to have gone to famine
In a season recurring from wind:
It would not turn.

Into a deep snow in sleep
I shook again. If she could not beat
The lightness from her clothes,
It would become a layer
That eddied around in mouth,

Myriad, in everywhere. No
Animal stirs in the noiseless
Quick of a year of two winters,
But marrow:

Gristle of a bloated fish, roots
Split and cached, skin torn
From the hull of a boat
Long withdrawn from water.

IV.

Hers, a burial in damp
Sand by the springs. Through
December, willows green
There; alder bark reddens

Against late snow. Those
Dead too numerous; no loose
Entombments beneath
Scars of rock. Nothing roots

In the oldest graves—
Lichen lifts with a fingernail scrape.
Leave belongings piled:
The opaque white bead

Now unstrung, the unidentified
Fragment, ivory ferrule,
The small human figure
Carved of wood.

Insomnia at North

I shall yet have a long sleep
When the dark is at a stand
In the woods. The rocks
Along the ridge

Will no longer ring
Like bells, but will
Become simple, gray
And silent. I will be

Still then, and sleep
As night now sleeps,
Swaying the larch
Outside my window.

It is losing its needles.
Dry slivers of gold
Drop in the tall,
Sheltering grass.

These I shall hurry,
And envy their settle.

The Designation

I live brokenly and assemble together
Weakly—from long bone of the arm, hip
Rollicking in its socket, and the jaw,

Its brux. From the lip of a wooden
Bowl carved from the knot of a limb
Drifted, my name was given on water

And laid down like hail upon my tongue.
It's become a bewilderment of white—
It snows. It does snow. It is snowing.

Variable at Prime

It was never a speedy alchemy—
It was a desolate town
That conquered me. I lifted

My hands to my head;
They shook. It was all over.
To obscure my path, I lit a fire.

Everything about me
Seemed to be toppling over.
The waves had begun their break

Into whitecaps. I crossed in fog.
Rivulets link lake to river.
He would like to go out

Towards the ocean,
Calmer, to see me fall easy,
And easier now.

Proper

A blue tusk, a petrifying blue—there is only
One way in which everything goes wrong.

This the raw tooth that would not rot,
What is left of the mammoth. Mineral

Leached from snowmelt, a deep blue
From vivianite, a phosphorescent blue.

A stain of slow excavation, of resurfacing
From ground bruised, bursts from cold.

It is a near station. I wanted to grow
Sound, but perhaps have strayed—

Drawn to dusk again, thinned by tension,
A bark ivory, dentine sloughed away.

Stative

I.

Along the hillside whorls of wind: I collect
Anemone, blown into a two-week peak

As Grass-of-Parnassus' small bog star
Throngs the marsh below.

I pick these flowers for weather,
To ferment and powder.

I do not know their cure, heal or sour,
Or if it is my name again written
One thousand times, grove upon grove.

II.

The bucket of a man pouring water,
A quarterly moon dips low.

Fish slip from the seine: it is time
To depart. As morning nears,
Ursa Major's last light trails.

III.

Who would not dream a year of two winters,
All dullness and narrow entrance?

What a mean thing, the horizon,
So open-mouthed at gap
And close of day. It drowns a thin disc
Of sun from its height of one thumb's width
At arm's length. We can measure
Its meanness.

IV.

An odor of
Ledum twisted in grip—

Dusk placed like a seal over liquid hours.
A cogged wheel pulls the tide near, away from shore.

V.

The water drained away
Reveals a flat land of grasses.

I began to miss one of the small bones
In my hand and it hurt.

On the Border of Speech

I did not swim under the water
Deliberately, though my eyes
Were pieces of ice as I plunged
Below its surface. I do not

Have a large heart. I am turning
My head to look up at the sky
That holds no stars. To the east
There hangs an isolated cloud

Of dust or smoke; perhaps
It is descending upon a place
That has many ravens. At night,
Sometimes, I hear them.

Here, the man is hammering.
I thought I had given the world
To him again, how sad instead
That he is hurt, that his sorrow

Has formed an impossible cluster.

Off Course

I.

A drag in the wake
Of a skeleton path
On water—
What can be said of
The small degree?

II.

With its unfixedness
March is difficult.
There was a map
I carried.

III.

I think it is time again.
Clear night, raised
Emblems

Of a man adrift.

Ruins

A pebble of humid air here
At Pilgrim Hot Springs where the first
Yet return to open water early.
A flight of cottonwood flush upwards,
Or, peregrines arc courses above the sloughs.
Each fissured surface shifts level.
What I thought light now
A premonition. What the fledged

Require weighs to the balance, to
Instinct. To the carved
Ivory orb, the tedium
Of form orphaned:
The drought settling
In your right hand.

Declining the City

Altogether elsewhere summer slips under its horizon.
Burst from the first frost, cloudberries embarrass
Rud-orange. Toughening beneath a clump of earth,
Moss campion's rough taproot gilds,
Calloused edible, too. For all of hunger,
Yarrow grows obdurate, brown on the stalk:

A gauntlet to winter. Ice spindles in the dry crown.
In departure, moulted geese blanket the lakes
With their shed feathers.

Here: multifoliate night, vapor-lit.
I've beat into leaf, a thin plate.

A Proposal

If weather
        and rock and moss.
If a flurry of white against the space
Where water undercuts the bank.
And herring roe clouds
        and gathers on boughs
Of blue spruce moored to shore . . .

A present of four deer, petty game,
Moves quiet and invisibly through trees.

Green wood grows from old roots,
Seals sleep on their backs, salt-borne,

And brightness on the horizon
Gives of a presence of ice on the ocean.

Let us turn the intestines inside out
        and eat them.

Anchorage

How rapidly the tide turned, turns.
Still, turning now, gray wash and silt
Pivots on a finger of foam.

One could count time in its long
Trough, or lose it altogether:

Winter may thicken the air
Earlier than expected. Or,

An inflection in the shadow
Of the long crest is an increment,
And a small variation.

With it, we are joined, and continue.
A sharp-shinned hawk now wheels

Overhead, as each spring tends,
And shows its white underbelly.

Placer

All salt and palms from the thin wrists
Down: mercury rolled in our fingers,
And heavy, rolled in dry mouths.

Grown sick of myth there, the word itself
Always catching and kenning
In the wrong tense, flashing back at us

A quick-silvered horizon—
The world and word a round heaved
And swelled thing, a grave sheen of shapes

Changing while countless sands
Of countless rivers converge and convey
Nothing of the long passage, though stopping

And sluicing and quicking unearth
What the earth itself would not let pass,
Yielding a yellow metal, ore

From the red sand coursed back
To the sea—a rushing, an amalgam,
A poison, an alloy. We're bound now,

Prospector, you've worked our shore.
We were children, once abundant

In the wake of your leaving.

Building the Boats

Yellow-lit beneath stretched
Skins, we play at bones,

Dig for ocher from clayey soil
To stain puffin bills for dance mitts.
They redly shake the sound of rain.

Downriver, cords of light hum,
Tobacco-smoked and hung
With salmon. Intervals of storm

Wash logs along the red-sanded
Shore before the tailings:

These you cut and steam,
Bend for frames.

Exit Glacier

The sea has called
For its slow quiescence,

A return from blue-white
Sleep to green-blue rough.

Threads of thick water
Make this valley new;

We are given its retreat,
A detraction in shale.

It follows, as surely as I
Had wanted to reach you:

Protected by a thing deeper
Than affection, more jagged.

Stray and Error

I.

Against the surface of night a rough
Red fury of morning, its bright mirror
Of dusk and its many angers.

                                It is mine,
It is brought around below a place
Of great sleep, or wakefulness.

II.

Like the stubble of the dry racks,
Fish carcasses ruin the water's edge.

I could not contain this stray, this error.

III.

The near mountains ring to form a wall.

I am fickle. Against the light I pull back.
It is of a long duration, a promontory
Along a tributary river. It is a brightness
That trails and passes the dark.

I do not know whether I should right or err,
Or retreat into those narrow valleys—

IV.

A tangle of branches in winter bud—
Dormant, quiescent in this season.

Above the ridge they are raised and dark.
They dream the symptom of a question.

I would not contain the light
Differently, between the ranges—

V.

The day itself a broken habit:
It should have sung the hours in order
From the first one on.

VI.

Rough against the shore, the wind is mine,
Commanding me in error.

The History of Two

We may as well stop here, tinder-dry
With ice too rough for hauling
Where falling oars falling through air
Once forgot tomorrow.

Failing to recall a flowering
Of shrub-birch heights,
Montane clusters, a necklace
Of blooms overlooking a line

Of surf we can no longer hear—
Cross-cousin, turn away
From our contests of accuracy
To study a prediction

In the patterns of branches
Pushed down by heavy snow.

Ornament

In increasingly deep water I swam,
Searching for a slight curve
Of glossy, polished blue
Evened down
Into translucent milk-white:
A long, slender half arc
Half buried in sand.

In shallows
I'd gone about with a rake—
I leveled its teeth
Against the floor of the sea,
Sinking toward a fragile shell
Set with fine engravings,
Numerous and close.

Decreased to a gradual margin,
It was a sculpture
In incandescent language.
I could not find it. Perplexed
By kelp and mud,
And by the current
With its definite direction.

Ivu

It is the ice-shove, the thrust
Of tons piled against
The verge of the land.
In a dream

It becomes the waves'
Frozen, stopped crest.
Within its folds
I must find my mother.

I am to decipher
A jade lump
Inscribed with runes.
I must retrieve it.

It is not a dream.
It is an ice-scour
On the seabed.
It has smothered

A place of sleep in winter:
The mound a house
On the bluff
Overlooking the sea.

Its long entrance
A choked tunnel
Of ice, its lungs
Stuffed with soot

From the oil lamp,
Now extinguished.
There is no thaw
I cannot find her.

Clear Cut

Something along the power lines produces a hiss and pop
Between wire and blue glass. A near gurgle of water suggests
A stream eddying into a shallow, a nearer sky
Sunk to shadow, the path veering uphill between lower plants.

I do not know the way forward, only away.
A small clearing beckons, timber untrimmed and strewn.
Dust-covered roses attenuate through the fold of twig and bark,
They do not know what they earn against the soil—

They do not escape the jinx of time and place,
Its unspeakable counsel. They observe a secrecy
Unknown to us, a brief arrangement of color and pollen.
From red meal the swollen hip drops a barbed seed.

And Other Ruins

Shown fine striations
Of garnet and gneiss
From the earth's skin
Just begun to split:

I could hear you
Singing. Willows thicket
Where ribbons of wood
Slash from a rough

Piece of green timber:
Ours a lore based upon
The relation of magnitudes.
In it, the world shone.

Light splintered once,
Spooling across the sky.
Meanwhile, cool air stirs
The curtain from a window,

Lifts voices in a motion
Of voices, and would again.

Laid In

I trace our path along the edge of the double,
Interlocking lake. The sky folding
Over itself, gray on white, and lit distantly.
It seemed then that something would fall.

Though I had not yet abandoned the promise of snow
In such a season, you could not even take note
Of a shift in the weather. Innocent, too,

Of the shadow between ranges, the air filling
With windblown silt, and darkening.

It was a way out. Ringing the water,
Grasses abound above their silent understory
Of mosses. The ash, fixed, is in its fine silence.

Antistrophic

A new angle of light this evening,
South—south
West, shadows cast upward bough upon bough
Also in disagreement. Another
Would mutter green
Amidst the black scrag of dense limbs
But already the light is fading
And contrary.

Instead of out, I am in,
Trying at the old habit of imperfect definition
As well as the less familiar,
Between falling gold

Trees I have learned not to name

And gold pulled
Of the sun as it fails.

Two: Otherwise, Sky

The Prodigy

This is a room that squalls with absence.

Nothing more could bring you back. Once
You were cursed in tragedy, as loosely hung

As smoke that had surrendered and spun
Toward the ceiling. I have made a close

Inventory of the ways in which I succumb
To long grass standing in winter: suppose

There might be a clearing, as I have done.
Suspect an abrupt miracle. As it sways,

The body is caught at the tangled root again,
It is caught at the end, again, against the day.

In a room in which you're found at every margin,
Forgetting you is nothing but a long discipline.

At Bridal Veil Rocks

I have laid hold of a hunger. I had
Skinned myself and extracted a splinter.

He shoots low and fails to reach.
Inside of my coat I fold
My arms. I omit you.

Elsewhere, a body inflects
High above the waterline.
The sun bows low, hides
As from an animal while stalking.

I am remorseful and have moved
To another dwelling. I turn over,
Change, and repent, wanting

That which is more valuable. With
Hope of finding an instrument for boring,

I heap stones to stand on, and in this way
Manage to make a hole in the roof.

On Eating before Hunting

When he went out in the morning,
His belly filled with dried fish,
Skin and all. Nothing surfaced for him.

He went home just as the sun
Made fire with flint. Two others
He saw going out in their boats,
Towing a bearded seal.

Over toward the end of the land
They went, as if rounding a bend.
He was almost sent around,
Foremost to name them.

It would not be understandable
Would they be stopped.
In a great hurry they untied
What they were towing.

The Greenland Mummies

I carry teeth lodged in the roof
Of my mouth, embedded at all angles.
They forbid a simple and direct reading.

They are small and misshapen.
To remove them, a rough
Surgery is scheduled.

Short shins and long thighs
Have sent me on a far fetch,
My feet covered with skins.

They too have borne me
Through sleep, a long journey
Against the dry wind

To this small human activity of survival.

Three Masks

I.

I have seen it, the mask of the badlands,
Our wilderness uninhabitable:

A disc with one round eye,
Three trailing feathers
About the temples and crown,
Hair pouring forth
From the open mouth.

The left eye a crescent,
A resistance to light.

A narrow red band of ocher
Around the white spruce face,
It brings sickness. It grants
The carcass of an animal
Drifted to shore.

II.

Reviviscence,
Shallowly excavated wood
Shaped by fire.

The large eyes
Irregular, rounded,

Charred and pierced through.

The wearer would
Grasp this through his teeth,
A thin ledge between labrets.

Its rough nose hangs down
Above a groove,
Below the nostrils

A drawn line.
It is a death-head.

III.

It is a loon swimming
On the surface of the water,

The head and neck
Fastened to the body by a peg.

They are a dull dark blue
Flecked with white—
They reign from the chin.

A wedge of a mouth.
Set above are oblique

Oval nostrils,
One judging eye.

Two wings marked
In pieces of wood
Affixed by root.

Drawn on the back
Is a face, eyes hooded
In snow goggles.

Hell is a place of accident.

Traveler's Rest

Pewter medals
And mirrors stowed

Heavy in the bow
Of your craft.

You have mapped
The shoals in the river,

I rise up like a road
Between its banks,

A bit of rough flannel
Between us. Though

I have at long last
Lost sight of you,

I am not telling you
New lies.

The nameable world
Ends. You are still

Breathing, lungs
Filling with self-praise.

Variations on an Admonition

I have played with the skulls of seals
And feigned them to be children.

I will tell you of the black spot
Constantly before me—

I had tried hard to make land,
But the coast has altogether vanished.

I ask that you keep your eyes shut
Until the sound of the swarm

Above has passed, that you mind not
A certain brightness. After all,

I have whittled you into life-size—
I will divide you into many men

With time for me to gather
The bones of all sorts of animals

And stir life into them.

The Relation

Midday walks on water; this thin peninsula
Swallows whole into sand its advance. A tall
Marsh grass overthrown with the odor

Of salt gives way to willow and alder
At land's edge. This is the beginning,
Or the end, or the plain ratio

Between these two distances.
The day is spun into wide use,
Expansive in its completeness,

Clear in its refrain.
Among the blades blowing
Down, broken, and blown back

Up again, I did not know
That you would lose this coherence.
Apportioned under the sun,

I looked for the girl with braids
Long as her arms, and find you,
Who had found me alone.

Animal Figurine

Two identical pools
Of tobacco-ash and blood—
Gunpowder would

Black the eyes
Of a seal carved of ivory
If provisions had not run so low

During an ill-omened
Overwinter. It is
Just as—

Against the bleached bone
Of the body, the storm
In its long hour—

Burnt fuel. The fixed
Discs of eye raised
In low relief. Not the replica

Of the solstice to scale,
But a focus of distance
Admitting light.

Lost Season

This is not the way,
Bloomed intact through such small beginnings.
The constellation was always mapped on the shell itself.

The Slate Fields

This was our private hemisphere,
A sheltered place, and one in which
I was not terror, and you were

Not lonely. A distant sky, a tired
Wattle. Entrusted to each as cold,
Abundant disease, we made a terrible

Edifice. You have seen one tree
Swim. I have been deceitful,
And in many things. I have

Had a careless tone. Please pretend
To love the small sign of my departure,
That I am one among the vague

Number swallowed whole.

Variable at Nightfall

The wind through the bare trees
A sea of knives.

The near mountain blue,
And bald with snow.

The carving in my hand
Shows half-walrus, half-bear.

They must turn always
From each other.

I wonder what I had
Watched for,

If the weather
Had told me something

That I did not already know.
Now, as the wind rises,

I will not follow it.

•

Withdraw

To the south of those who live south of us—
I will visit unknown men, hunt up the invisible
Behind the women.

It is both a bluster and a promise,
The day immature, blunt in its newness.
I do not know what steals me

Above the spines of mountains.
I trespass to hear the sound of the sea,
Its resemblance to a summit of wind.

Child, I pare off. The swallows
Have disappeared into their banks
And emerged as wolves. Expect

A bird of beak and tooth, the steep
Fetch, the sigh of new-formed ice.

Tributary

Just beyond a bend in the river
A soup of two birds

Looses roots from the mud
Of the iron-red marsh.

They create a current of water.
Otherwise white in the white light

One stretches its rust-stained neck,
Tips up to feed. Pale irises rise

Amid the swan pair
Nesting between alder-lined streams.

It is let loose. It has gone to ruin.
It breathes, uttering life. Against

The southern sky the mountains sawtooth
In their licit coldness. Below

Is their labor, repeating.

The Slip

Kept relic, still visible at neap tide:
Wheels, the long arm of a dredge,
Iron cogs, a boiler punctured through.

Inland, a line of rust. A locomotive
Sits unhitched, its splayed cars
Fixed into a forest of themselves.

Of struck gold, of silt stranded—

This long-relinquished railroad
Would not ferry it all away.
Rains of grayling ascend,

Striking against slow waters.
We are miles from the line's
Heavy-timbered terminus
And its rock-filled dock.

Nelson's Curio

An assemblage fine
And hidden: wooden
Shafts tipped with flint,
Baleen boxes, women's

Ivory-handled knives,
Shuttles notched in bone
And sinew, willow bark
Nets, and bodkins'

Round, slender rods
Terminating in the
Heads of unfamiliar
Animals, offered as if

To say, we are strong,
We do not steal.

Nix

The trees are no longer in new leaf: they lie still,
Secretly weighted by day.

It could be the handful of glass pills
Tucked behind a row of books

Left by one who walked out, our dusk
Managed into a fine obsidian truth.

I could have done worse, a smaller wrecking
Away. It was not a mistake I made, not

The accidental birds blown by storm, but the
Sound of fowl startled from their nests. Black

Birds wheeled above a green river.
A plow followed to sand coated with ice

Through a pass filling with snow,
It doesn't seem to be coming any nearer.

Five Stops

I.

A bloom of influenza
Resistant to a blue
Mass, a salve. Rasp
And catarrh.

II.

Him pressing
A brown moth
Beneath the heel,
Grinding it to powder.

III.

Light like
A murre's egg
Thrown against
A wall.

IV.

The blown yolk
Blurs orange.
Speckled shell,
Thick albumin.

V.

That now burnt
Haunch of meat,
That mouthful,
That fur of the hare.

Fled to the Inlanders

I.

She happened to break a reindeer-horn
Needle belonging to her elder sister—

She cried down into a stone.

Who had been sent away for spoiling
His brother's snare would

Wife her with hides.

He would wade into a lake
And take the eider birds by stealth.

Betrayed by ice and desertion,
She could smell the coast about her.

II.

One became a reindeer—
Another assumed the shape of a hare in winter.
One pulled the skin from his bones

But for the space between his eyes.
One danced so the house angled forward,
Lapsed and toppled.

One built a stone boat. Upriver,
If she could distinguish the earth,
It would not move.

One danced and flung himself down,
Transformed into glistening feldspar.
He rose up again in his proper shape.

One fell into a common rock.
Lifted, thrown: he split to pieces.

III.

Into vermin-filled
Boots they stuffed
Her bones, brief,
Below the ankle.

The straps tightened
About her, the skin
Dropped off
Her feet and legs.

Fallen into a swoon,
As them she
Had become as nimble,
Assembled to follow.

IV.

She had longed for her relatives—

Though he would not follow her brothers
As they watched above the breathing

Holes of seals, he would ask her father for a trap
And return all covered with ducks.

V.

A man in a mirage once let his forgotten love
Break from the branches
And thus be forgiven.

By this sullen movement, a bafflement of gravel,
His drawing close to dark
Had flown him free

Of past enchantments. She too, hopes to be let
From the brittle constellation,
                                        The barren dream.

Birth at Safety Sound

The river rushes at break-up,
The weather moderated from a wind
Northeasterly and paralleling the shoreline.

She has adopted that which is diminishing
In light, she has lost and redeemed it.
The things washed against the shore

Are knocking, touch ground, and settle in.
She has protected him, forgotten
The name of the messenger. It rakes

Against and lies with her. It is creased,
Corrugated, a cut path through the trees,
Severed. Like one who is back there,

Behind her, away from shore. Landwards,
Mountainwards. There is a small cry,
An exclamation, a warning—

It splits like a sole from a shoe.
Loosens like two things frozen together.

The White Night Falling

When it becomes another summer,
She is still hurt. It has come
Down upon her.

In one of their two tents
On the sand, she oversleeps
And wakes between a footprint

And a mountain
Only to step on a nail.
She will take a boat

To the river tomorrow.
Together, the game animals
Travel in another way

Toward a specific destination.
They are scarce. The ocean
Rises, trims their shore.

Haunt

While crossing new snow in spring
Seeking greens, the far cape swam

Across the water. Each
Of its creeks grew legible . . .

In a swarm of small gray birds,
A cormorant with two heads.

A voice calling echoed closer,
Flocking and loud. Beneath

The black rock atop the island
In switched leads through thickening

Snow, one girl dispelled another
From that place. All sound

Gusts away in its bright season . . .
It is a groove in the handle of a thing

That cannot be lifted. A false
Companion shunned

Had removed herself. All alone
Has she come here, from where,

For that black rock rattling terribly, again.

The Cormorant Hunter's Wife

Black birds luster in sleep above a rough
Sea, and he is all suspension from a length
Of rope before descending to snap ten
Long necks, one after another. Cormorants

In death are just lustrous: swollen from a day's
Plunging, distended with fish. He wants
To own his weighty bounty upward,
But she in cunning cuts his cord and turns

To the other in her husband's falling.
Implausible travels from a scar of rock,
And a return that needs no telling.
Is it her failing: the cormorant hunter's wife

Feels no ill will all winter until the spring,
When, in a glutton's plumpness with her black
Hair lustered, he buries her beneath a sum of stones
And himself plunges with the downdrafts under.

Theories of Migration

As if to start over,
The mouth of the bay opens seaward.

I will never sleep here,
Bounded by interrupted spruce.
Beyond the tell of low pressure

A few movements recede
Into black manganese and basalt—

Trap rock. The palm of a child.
A line of deer, the drought fed.
Trace their bright configuration

And move through barrens
In the hold of different mountains.

Due North

I should have my hood on—
Already there are rumors of darkness.
I should see the stones set before me,
Giving passage toward a place
Of complex nostalgias. And now
Should see the scree falling

Endlessly from the mountain's summit,
Falling on the recessive plain.
It is a private place, a wilderness
In practice. I am told that I should look
For a roof in rain, for a river
Spilt down to tongues of ice.

I shall start all together. As hollow
As a drum, the ground sounds—
It summons, repeats beneath me.
It is as intact and unchangeable
As the seven stars spun into position
When the day, which takes hours to fade,

Has dropped away in its small mist.

Dust in June

A liquid hour that I miss, the lengthened evening
Given to a sullen morning slept through in dark—
A motionlessness

                past, a gathering of moss for wicks.
The summer yet come around in arrows
Prepared for the enemies we have made of ourselves.

Each of the aspen bends as if before
A storm, the leaves turned from deep-green
Side to silver. As if nickels rain down to dust
In June, the air gone metallic. A truth

                      to bind, drag
Over ground toward water, flense and clean.

I learn surfaces breaking. I cannot get
To the line on the horizon where the first cloud
Holds the air on its fingers.

Tiŋmiat

Black bird,
I have named you.

I have known
Your interdiction.
The otherwise

Sky was profuse
In its whiteness,
A confusion of

Snow come again
Into snow. Raven
Who would be made

Of wax, pitch.
In this way grow
Fast in my mind.

Biographical Note

Joan Kane is Inupiaq with family from King Island and Mary's Igloo, Alaska. She earned her bachelor's degree from Harvard College and her MFA from Columbia University. Her honors include the 2004 John Haines Award from Ice Floe Press, a 2007 individual artist award from the Rasmuson Foundation, the 2009 Connie Boochever Fellowship from the Alaska State Council on the Arts, a 2009 National Native Creative Development Program grant, the 2010 Alaska Conservation Foundation's Native Writers on the Environment award, and a 2009 Whiting Writers' Award. Along with her husband and sons, she lives in Anchorage, Alaska.